T0365349

Little Gospel Fingers Play Spirituals

Stories and Arrangements by

VIVIAN JOHNSON

Illustrations by

KENYA GIBBONS

Scripture quotations marked NIV are taken from
the *Holy Bible, New International Version®. NIV®.*
Copyright © 1973, 1978, 1984 by International Bible
Society. Used by permission of Zondervan. All rights
reserved. [Biblica]

Copyright © 2015 by Vivian Johnson . 725481
Library of Congress Control Number: 2015917283

ISBN: Softcover   978-1-5144-1867-3
         Hardcover   978-1-5144-1868-0
         EBook   978-1-5144-1866-6

All rights reserved. No part of this book may
be reproduced or transmitted in any form or by
any means, electronic or mechanical, including
photocopying, recording, or by any information storage
and retrieval system, without permission in writing from
the copyright owner.

Print information available on the last page

Rev. date: 04/25/2016

To order additional copies of this book, contact:
Xlibris
1-888-795-4274
www.Xlibris.com
Orders@Xlibris.com

Little Gospel Fingers
Play Spirituals

Stories and Arrangements by
VIVIAN JOHNSON

CONTENTS

A Note from the Arranger

This collection of spirituals was arranged and complied over several years for my piano students. They enjoyed playing the spirituals and often asked questions about their meaning. So, I have included the story behind the spirituals with information about how and why they were sung. I only used a few words in dialect because I wanted my students to understand what they were reading.

Spirituals and their stories were passed down from generation to generation as slaves sang them while working, worshiping and taking care of their children. My aunt, Katie Ewing Diggs (1875-1975), told me stories about slavery that her mother (my great grandmother), Phyllis Robinson Ewing (1845-1927), had told her. As a child, I learned a lot about the past from Aunt Katie and I understood more about spirituals after hearing Bible stories in Sunday school classes where Aunt Katie was one of my teachers.

I am happy and excited to share this music because most of my students did not know about Black Spirituals. However, all of my students enjoy playing them. They especially like the lively, energetic accompaniment that enhances several of the melodies. I believe others will enjoy the spirituals too.

With warmest wishes,

Vivian M. Johnson

Steal Away

arr. Vivian M. Johnson

The Stories behind the Spirituals

Songs were created by slaves as they worked long, hard hours on the plantations. These songs came to be known as Negro Spirituals. The spirituals were religious and often told Bible stories or expressed the desire to go to heaven. They were comforting and expressed hope for a better day. Slaves not only sang to help ease the physical and mental pain of slavery, many of their songs gave messages. They provided clues on when to escape and gave direction to runaway slaves. One such spiritual is "Steal Away". The verses tell the slaves to run during a storm.

Chorus: Steal away, steal away, steal away to Jesus.

              Steal away, steal away home.

              I ain't got long to stay here.

Verse 1:   Green trees a-bendin', poor sinner stands a-tremblin'

              The trumpet sounds within-a-my soul

              I ain't got long to stay here.

Verse 2:   My Lord, He calls me, He calls me by the thunder

              The trumpet sounds within-a-my soul

              I ain't got long to stay here.

Verse 3:   My Lord, He calls me, He calls me by the lightening

              The trumpet sounds within-a-my soul

              I ain't got long to stay here.

The spirituals in this book have stories behind them, too. Read the stories, play the music and enjoy the spirituals.

"Get On Board"

"Get On Board" is a spiritual that tells about the Underground Railroad. It was not a real railroad; it was a network of white and free black people who provided places for runaway slaves to hide. They helped the slaves get to the north where they would be free. The Underground Railroad was actually homes, barns and churches, trees in the forest, rivers, and paths through the woods. They also traveled by train, wagon and boat. The slaves traveled any way possible to secretly escape to the north and to freedom.

This spiritual encourages slaves to escape by taking the Underground Railroad. At the end of the refrain the words are: "Get on board little children, there's room for many-a more".

Get On Board Little Children

(Accompaniment)

Arr. Vivian M. Johnson

Get On Board Little Children

Arr. Vivian M. Johnson

The Stories Behind the Spiritual

"All Night, All Day"

(Exodus 13:17-22, 14:5-20 NIV)

When God brought the children of Israel out of Egypt, He protected them from being captured and enslaved again. After the king of Egypt was told that the Israelites had left Egypt, Pharaoh and his army went to catch them. By day the angel of the Lord went in front of the Israelites in a pillar of cloud to lead them. By night the angel of the Lord was behind them in a pillar of fire to give them light.

When the Israelites reached the Red Sea, they had no way to cross to the other side. Moses could hear Pharaoh's horses and chariots behind him. He prayed to the Lord and the Lord told him to raise his staff and stretch it out over the sea. When he stretched out his staff the waters divided and the Israelites came through on dry ground. Then the angel of God, who had been traveling in front of them, moved and went behind them. The pillar of cloud also moved from the front and stood behind them. It stood between them and the Pharaoh's army. All night the cloud made darkness on the Egyptian army and light on the Israelites. All day the cloud of light guided them. God had sent an angel to watch over them and keep them safe from their enemies both night and day.

This spiritual reminded the runaway slaves that God was also watching over them 'all night and all day'... just as He had done for Moses and the Israelites.

All Night, All Day

Arr. Vivian M. Johnson

Soft and Gentle

All night, All day.

An - gels watch-ing o - ver me my Lord.

All night. All day.

An - gels watch- ing o - ver me.

Mary Had a Baby

arr. Vivian M. Johnson

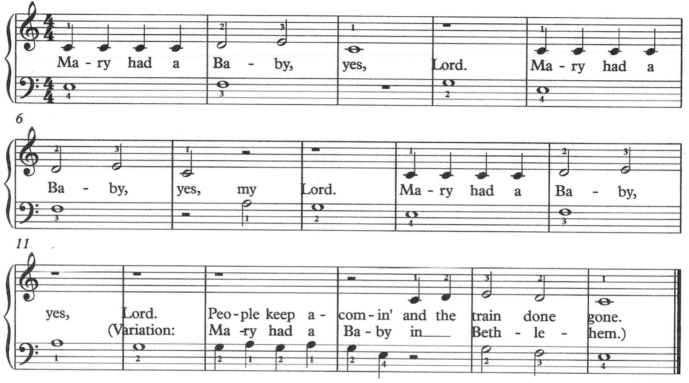

2. Where did she lay Him?   Yes Lord.
   Where did she lay Him?   Yes, my Lord.
   Where did she lay Him?   Yes Lord.
   People keep a-comin' and the train done gone.

3. Laid Him in a manger.   Yes Lord.
   Laid Him in a manger.   Yes, my Lord.
   Laid Him in a manger.   Yes Lord.
   People keep a-comin' and the train done gone.

4. What did she name Him?   Yes Lord.
   What did she name Him?   Yes, my Lord.
   What did she name Him?   Yes Lord.
   People keep a-comin' and the train done gone.

5. Named Him King Jesus.   Yes Lord.
   Named Him King Jesus.   Yes, my Lord.
   Named Him King Jesus.   Yes Lord.
   People keep a-comin' and the train done gone.

"Mary Had A Baby"

(Matthew 1:18-25, 2:1-15 and Luke 1:26-45, 2:1-20 NIV)

"Mary Had A Baby" is based on the story of Jesus' birth, also known as the Christmas story. A star hovered over the manger where Jesus was born. The book of Matthew tells that the Wise Men had to follow the star to find Jesus and that Herod tried to trick them into telling where Jesus was born. Luke shares the story of the angels singing at His birth and the shepherds coming to worship Him.

"Mary Had A Baby" is sung in "call and response" style. In this singing style, which came from Africa, the leader sings the first part and the group answers. Below is an example of how Mary Had a Baby was sung.

Call	Response
Leader: Mary had a baby	**Group:** Yes Lord
Leader: Mary had a baby	**Group:** Yes my Lord
Leader: Mary had a baby	**Group:** Yes Lord
All: Mary had a baby in Bethlehem	

Sometimes the leader would make up a verse using secret codes. This kept the slaves informed without the master suspecting anything. The leader sang messages about runaways, the Underground Railroad and events in daily life.

"Swing Low, Sweet Chariot"

"Swing Low, Sweet Chariot" is a spiritual with a double meaning. At first it is easy to see that the singer is talking about going to heaven. But, 'chariot' was also a code word for wagon or buggy. And 'home' or 'heaven' meant the north or freedom. Escape plans were secretly made and were passed on by word of mouth. When messages were sent through songs, the slaves would know the signs and signals for the best time to run. A common way to help slaves escape was to hide them under crops or clothes that were headed to town or another plantation.

There are many interesting stories about how slaves escaped to freedom. One story tells about the slave Henry "Box" Brown and how he escaped by mailing himself in a box. Another is about a married couple, Ellen and William Craft. Their escape was an adventure because Ellen was disguised as a white male with William posing as her slave.

Slaves risked their lives trying to escape. Many made it to freedom and many did not. Verses in "Swing Low, Sweet Chariot" show that slaves never gave up the dream of being free.

Verse 1

"I looked over Jordan and what did I see?
Comin' for to carry me home...
A band of angels coming after me,
Comin' for to carry me home..."

Verse 2

"I'm sometimes up and sometimes down.
Comin' for to carry me home...
But still my soul is heaven bound.
Comin' for to carry me home..."

Verse 3

"If you get there before I do
Comin' for to carry me home...
Tell all my friends I'm comin', too
Comin' for to carry me home..."

Swing Low Sweet Chariot
(Accompaniment)

Arr. Vivian M. Johnson

Swing Low Sweet Chariot

With feeling
Play one octave higher

Arr. Vivian M. Johnson

"Go Down Moses"

(Exodus: Chapters 3 through 12 NIV)

God heard the prayers of the children of Israel when they were enslaved by the Egyptians. He called Moses to go down to Egypt and tell Pharaoh to let His people go. Moses didn't think he could do what God told him to do; so, God sent his brother Aaron to Egypt with him and they told Pharaoh what God had said.

Pharaoh did not want to allow the Israelites to go. He made their work harder. So, Moses was given the power to perform many signs to show Pharaoh that he was sent by the Lord God of Abraham, Isaac and Jacob. Moses turned his staff into a serpent, made his hand leprous and turned water into blood, but Pharaoh did not allow them to go. Then, God sent many plagues on the Egyptians. A few of them were frogs, gnats, flies, locusts and darkness, but Pharaoh still would not allow them to go.

The Lord told Moses to have each family of Israelites prepare a lamb (or goat) for slaughter; then take the blood and put it on the side and top of the doorframe of their houses. They needed to eat the meat that night. On that same night the Lord said He would pass through Egypt and strike down every first born of man and animal. The blood on the doorframe would be a sign that Israelites were living there and the Lord would pass over that house and spare them from death. On the night of the Passover, there was moaning and crying coming from all the houses without blood on the doorframe. Even the Pharaoh's first born was struck down. But, all of the houses with the blood were passed over. The Israelites were spared from destruction. After the devastation during the "Passover", Pharaoh allowed the Children of Israel to go.

Slaves sang this spiritual because they were enslaved like the Israelites. They prayed and believed that God would set them free, also.

Go Down Moses

"Dry Bones"

(Ezekiel 37:1-14 NIV)

When the Israelites were captive in Babylon, they started worshiping idol gods. God wanted them to return to Him. So, through the Holy Spirit, God carried the prophet Ezekiel to the Valley of the Bones. God told Ezekiel that these bones were the people of Israel. He wanted Ezekiel to prophesy to the bones. The Lord said, "I will put My Spirit in them, they will live and settle in their own land".

While still in the spirit, Ezekiel prophesied to the bones and they came to life. After that, he knew he had to prophesy to the people of Israel so that they would return to the true and living God.

Slaves liked to sing action songs and humorous or amusing songs to lift their spirits. One of their favorites was "Dry Bones". They enjoyed singing the verses which named the bones in the order that they are connected. They often accompanied their singing by clapping their hands and stomping their feet. The men who were talented in making body rhythms would make the rhythms by slapping their hands on their chest and thighs. The body rhythms were adapted from a style of dance called Juba that slaves brought to America from Africa.

Dry Bones

Refrain   #1: Them bones, them bones, them dry bones.
Them bones, them bones, them dry bones.
Them bones, them bones, them dry bones.
Now hear the word of the Lord.

Verses:

1. The toe bone's connected to the foot bone,
The foot bone's connected to the ankle bone,
The ankle bone's connected to the leg bone.
Now hear the word of the Lord.

2. The leg bone's connected to the knee bone,
The knee bone's connected to the thigh bone,
The thigh bone's connected to the hip bone.
Now hear the word of the Lord.

3. The hip bone's connected to the back bone,
The back bone's connected to the neck bone,
The neck bone's connected to the head bone.
Now hear the word of the Lord.

Refrain   #2: Them bones, them bones gonna walk around.
Them bones, them bones gonna walk around.
Them bones, them bones gonna walk around.
Now hear the word of the Lord

Dry Bones

arr. Vivian M. Johnson

"Joshua Fought the Battle of Jericho"

(Joshua: Chapters 3, 5 and 6 NIV)

"Joshua Fought the Battle of Jericho" is taken from a Bible story. God chose Joshua to lead the Israelites to the Promised Land after Moses died. Joshua secretly sent spies to look at the land which was in the city of Jericho. The people of Jericho were afraid because they had heard how the Lord dried up the Jordan River so the Israelites could walk across. The king of Jericho was afraid, too. When he heard about the spies and that the Israelites were camped near Jericho, he stopped everyone from going out or coming in the city.

Joshua knew that the Lord would show him how to conquer the land. One day the Lord told Joshua to have all armed men march around the walls of Jericho for six days. On the seventh day they were to march around the city seven times with the priests blowing their trumpets. All of the people had to give a loud shout when the trumpets made a long blast. Then the walls would fall down.

Joshua and the Israelites obeyed God. They marched, blew the trumpets and shouted just as God had told them to do. Then they heard a very loud sound as 'the walls came tumbling down'. The institution of slavery was confining like the Jericho wall and the slaves wanted it to 'come tumbling down', too.

Joshua Fought the Battle of Jericho

Refrain

Joshua fought the battle of Jericho, Jericho, Jericho.
Joshua fought the battle of Jericho,
And the walls come tumbling down.

Verses:

1. You can talk about the men of Gideon,
   You can talk about the men of Saul,
   But there's none like good old Joshua
   At the battle of Jericho.

2. Up to the walls of Jericho,
   He marched with spear in hand
   "Go blow your ram horns," Joshua cried
   "'Cause the battle is in my hands!"

3. And then the ram horns began to blow
   The trumpets began to sound
   Joshua commanded the children to shout!
   And the walls come tumbling down

Joshua Fought the Battle Of Jericho

Arr. Vivian M. Johnson

(Accompaniment)

Joshua Fought the Battle of Jericho

Arr. Vivian M. Johnson

Fast and Lively
Play one octave higher

Josh - ua fought the bat - tle of - Je - ri - cho!

Je - ri - cho! Je - ri - cho!

Josh - ua fought the bat - tle of - Je - ri - cho!

And the walls came tumb - ling down!

29

When the Saints Go Marching In

Arr. Viviam M. Johnson

Happy March Tempo   (Accompaniment)

"When the Saints Go Marching In"

(Revelations 7:9-12 NIV)

"When the Saints Go Marching In" is based on an event that is recorded in the Bible. In the book of Revelations, John wrote that God allowed him to see Heaven in a dream. John saw a great multitude in Heaven. There were so many in that number, no one could count them. They were all tribes of people from every nation and they spoke in every language. They were dressed in white robes and held palm branches in their hands. The multitude was praising and worshiping God.

When slaves sang this spiritual, they were also singing about being in the number of slaves who escaped to freedom. They ended each verse with a short prayer: "Lord I want to be in that number, when the saints go marching in".

When the Saints Go Marching In

arr. Vivian M. Johnson

Happy March Tempo
Play one octave higher

Oh when the saints | go march-ing in, | oh when the

saints go march-ing in, | Lord I want to be in that

num-ber | when the saints go march-ing in.

References

Boatner, E. <u>Spirituals Triumphant – Old and New.</u> Nashville, Tenn.: Sunday School Publishing Board, National Baptist Convention, U.S.A., 1927

Seeger, R. C. <u>American Folk Songs for Christmas.</u> Garden City, New York: Doubleday & Company, Inc., 1953

The Holy Bible - Black Heritage Edition. Nashville, Tenn.: Today, Inc. 1976

Mom's Devotional Bible New International Version. Grand Rapids, Michigan: Zondervan Publishing House 1996

Townsend, W. A. <u>Gospel Pearls.</u> Nashville, Tenn.: Sunday School Publishing Board, National Baptist Convention, U.S.A., 1921

Aunt Katie Ewing Diggs (1875 – 1975) Oral History

Personal Knowledge

Printed in the United States
By Bookmasters